I0200666

A CourseGuide for

Evangelism
in a
Skeptical
World

Sam Chan

ZONDERVAN ACADEMIC

ZONDERVAN ACADEMIC

A CourseGuide for Evangelism in a Skeptical World

Copyright © 2019 by Zondervan

Requests for information should be addressed to:
Zondervan, *3900 Sparks Dr. SE, Grand Rapids, Michigan 49546*

ISBN 978-0-310-11050-7 (softcover)

All Scripture quotations, unless otherwise indicated, are taken from The Holy Bible, New International Version®, NIV®. Copyright © 1973, 1978, 1984, 2011 by Biblica, Inc.® Used by permission of Zondervan. All rights reserved worldwide. www.Zondervan.com. The "NIV" and "New International Version" are trademarks registered in the United States Patent and Trademark Office by Biblica, Inc.®

Any internet addresses (websites, blogs, etc.) and telephone numbers in this book are offered as a resource. They are not intended in any way to be or imply an endorsement by Zondervan, nor does Zondervan vouch for the content of these sites and numbers for the life of this book.

No part of this publication may be reproduced, stored in a retrieval system, or transmitted in any form or by any means — electronic, mechanical, photocopy, recording, or any other — except for brief quotations in printed reviews, without the prior permission of the publisher.

Printed in the United States of America

CONTENTS

Introduction

Welcome to *A CourseGuide for Evangelism in a Skeptical World*. These guides were created for formal and informal students alike who want to engage deeper in biblical, theological, or ministry studies. We hope this guide will provide an opportunity for you to grow not only in your understanding, but also in your faith.

How to Use This Guide

This guide is meant to be used in conjunction with the book *Evangelism in a Skeptical World* and its corresponding videos, *Evangelism in a Skeptical World Video Study*. After you have read each chapter in the book and watched the accompanying video lesson, the materials in this guide will help you review and assess what you have learned. Application-oriented questions are included as well.

Each CourseGuide has been individually designed to best equip you in your studies, but in general, you can expect the following components. Most CourseGuides begin every chapter with a "You Should Know" section, which highlights key terminology, people, and facts to remember. This section serves as a helpful summary for directing your studies. Reflection questions, typically two to three per chapter, prompt you to summarize key points you've learned. Discussion questions invite you to an even deeper level of engagement. Finally, most chapters will end with a short quiz to test your retention. You can find the answer key to each quiz at the bottom of the page following it.

For Further Study

CourseGuides accompany books and videos from some of the world's top biblical and theological scholars. They may be used independently, or in small groups or classrooms, offering quality instruction to equip students for academic and ministry pursuits. If you would like to engage in further study with Zondervan's CourseGuides, the full lineup may be viewed online. After completing your studies with *A CourseGuide for Evangelism in a Skeptical World*, we recommend moving on to *A CourseGuide for Apologetics at the Cross*, *A CourseGuide for Cultural Apologetics*, and *A CourseGuide for Seeking Allah, Finding Jesus*.

CHAPTER 1

A Theology of Evangelism

You Should Know

- The New Testament uses the noun *euangelion* to refer to the story about Jesus Christ.

- Three Greek verb forms of communicating the gospel: *martureō* ("to testify" or "bear witness"); *kērussō* ("to herald"); *propheteuō* ("to prophesy")

- External call: the evangelist's natural means of communicating the gospel

- Internal call: the Holy Spirit's supernatural personal agency that illuminates the hearer's understanding of the gospel

- Locution: the act of saying something; the meaning — sense and reference — of what is said

- Illocution: the act in saying something; the force — the action performed — of what is said

- Perlocution: the act by saying something; the effect — the result — of what is said

- *Metanoia*: change of heart, character, and disposition

- *Epistrophē*: a complete turn-around that has both negative and positive aspects

- The three aspects of faith: propositional knowing (*notitia*); assent (*assensus*); personal trust (*fiducia*)

- The three models of conversion: the Prodigal Son (Luke 15:11–32); Saul (Acts 9:1–30); Timothy (2 Tim. 1:5; 3:15)

- The three models of evangelism: Lydia (Acts 16:13–15); the slave girl (Acts 16:16–20); the Jailer (Acts 16:22–34)

Reflection Questions

1. Summarize the gospel according to storytellers.

2. Explain the concepts of "evangelism" and "conversion" in your own words.

3. Which of Timothy Keller's three models for evangelism in Acts 16 do you identify most with? How can you use that model in evangelism?

Discussion Question

1. What are the differences between the *external* call and the *internal* call of the gospel? How does the Holy Spirit factor into this discussion? What is the relationship between God's work and the human evangelist's efforts to convert a soul to Christianity?

Quiz

1. Which of the following is not one of the Greek words related to "gospel"?

    a) *Euangelion*
    b) *Euangelistēs*
    c) *Euthus*
    d) *Euangelizō*

2. Which "sense" of evangelism communicates the gospel to both believers and non-believers?

    a) Broad
    b) Narrow

   c) Gnomic

   d) Aphoristic

3. Which "sense" of evangelism communicates the gospel to non-believers with the intent of urging them to believe?

   a) Broad

   b) Narrow

   c) Gnomic

   d) Aphoristic

4. New Testament exegetes answer the question "What is the gospel?" by:

   a) Prescribing structured biblical ideas for our contemporary settings

   b) Tracing the story of what God has done, and continues to do, to save his people

   c) Describing what New Testament writers say about the gospel

   d) Interacting with the various Greco-Roman religions' doctrine of salvation

5. Systematic theologians answer the question "What is the gospel?" by:

   a) Prescribing structured biblical ideas for our contemporary settings

   b) Tracing the story of what God has done, and continues to do, to save his people

   c) Describing what New Testament writers say about the gospel

   d) Interacting with the various Greco-Roman religions' doctrine of salvation

6. Biblical theologians answer the question "What is the gospel?" by:

   a) Prescribing structured biblical ideas for our contemporary settings

   b) Tracing the story of what God has done, and continues to do, to save his people

   c) Describing what New Testament writers say about the gospel

   d) Interacting with the various Greco-Roman religions' doctrine of salvation

7. God's supernatural work is the _____ of regeneration.

    a) Instrumental means

    b) Natural means

    c) Cause

    d) Force

8. The natural work of someone hearing the gospel is the _____ of regeneration.

    a) Instrumental means

    b) Natural means

    c) Cause

    d) Force

9. Which of the following is NOT one of the Reformers' aspects of faith?

    a) Propositional knowing (*notitia*)

    b) Able not to sin (*possē non peccarē*)

    c) Assent (*assensus*)

    d) Personal trust (*fiducia*)

10. Which of the following could NOT be used to describe one of the models of conversion?

    a) Rebel

    b) Zealot

    c) Carnal Christian

    d) Believer-since-infancy

ANSWER KEY

1. C, 2. A, 3. B, 4. C, 5. A, 6. B, 7. C, 8. A, 9. B, 10. C

CHAPTER 2

Everyday Evangelism

You Should Know

- Plausibility structures: accepted beliefs, convictions, and understandings that determine the plausibility of a truth claim

- Plausibility structures come from community; experience; and facts, evidence, and data

- Noumenal: the realm of God, ethics, and values

- Phenomenal: the realm of facts, evidence, and data

- The "layers" of conversation: values, interests, and worldviews

- Things we should do during an evangelistic conversation: listen, understand, and empathize

- The elements that make up a story: personal events and a story-telling grid

- The movements of a story: introduction, body, conclusion

- A story's specific functions: introduction, definition of mission, body, bridge, climax, and denouement

- When doing evangelism, it is necessary for the witnesser to provide a safe atmosphere for the witnessee — one in which their opinions will not be "shut down."

Reflection Questions

1. Choose one of the strategies that speaks the most to your situation. In what ways can you apply this strategy to your life?

2. Explain the Kantian *Noumenal-Phenomenal* divide. How does it relate to the opposing realms of the sacred and the profane?

3. Explain each of the three movements of a story, including their specific functions, in your own words.

Discussion Question

1. Consider the six strategies for everyday evangelism. Briefly explain each strategy and describe the strengths and weaknesses of each.

Quiz

1. (T/F) Plausibility structures indicate the truth status (ontology) of a truth claim.

2. Which of the following is NOT a source for plausibility structures?
   a) Religion
   b) Community
   c) Experience
   d) Facts, evidence, and data

3. (T/F) Our community is very powerful in determining what we find believable or unbelievable.

4. Which of the following are Kant's separate realms of knowledge?
   a) Sacred
   b) Noumenal
   c) Profane
   d) Phenomenal
   e) A & C
   f) B & D

5. Which of the following are the three "layers" of conversation?
   a) Values
   b) Interests
   c) Worldviews
   d) All of the above

6. What are the three things we should do during an evangelistic conversation?

    a) Listen, understand, empathize

    b) Understand, think, debate

    c) Empathize, think, understand

    d) Listen, understand, debate

7. What are the two elements that make up a story?

    a) Personal events and public events

    b) A storytelling grid and a multi-point outline

    c) Personal events and a multi-point outline

    d) Personal events and a storytelling grid

8. What is/are the main "movement(s)" of a story?

    a) Introduction

    b) Body

    c) Conclusion

    d) All of the above

    e) None of the above

9. (T/F) If we tell our story as a story, then we can apply the Greek Rule of Threes.

10. (T/F) When telling a story about Jesus, it's necessary to resist the temptation to correct the hearer's answers in the interest of providing a "safe" atmosphere.

ANSWER KEY

1. F, 2. A, 3. T, 4. F, 5. D, 6. A, 7. D, 8. D, 9. T, 10. T

CHAPTER 3

How to Craft a Gospel Presentation

You Should Know

- What we do when we present the gospel: Present the gospel elements; use a set of coherent biblical metaphors to organize the elements (and leave out other biblical metaphors); be sharp, focused, penetrating, and to the point.

- Blocher's metaphors for sin: transgression, falling short, iniquity

- Three theological components to sin: internal, horizontal, and vertical

- Vertical manifestation of sin: offence against God, death, judgment

- Three biblical concepts of sin: breaking a law (guilt), defilement (unclean), and breaking relationships (shame)

- The shame and dishonor model of sin describes our failure to live up to God's objective standards for mankind.

- It is not a good idea to use the word "sin" because Jesus himself often doesn't use the word "sin" to describe sin and the meaning of the word "sin" has changed over time.

- Gospel presentations are focused summaries of the gospel. As such they must restrict themselves to some of the chief gospel metaphors.

- The six phases in Two Ways to Live: God is King; we reject God as King; God's punishment for rebellion is death and judgment; God so loved the world he sent his Son, Jesus Christ, into the world; God raised Jesus to life again as King of the world; we can live our way or God's way.

- Four Spiritual Laws' gospel presentation: God loves you and has a plan for your life; man is sinful and separated from God; Jesus Christ is God's only provision for man's sin; we must receive Jesus as Savior and Lord.

Reflection Questions

1. Explain one way the Bible uses to present the gospel message. What are this method's strengths? What are its weaknesses?

2. What is a fair way to judge a gospel presentation? Are there elements that must be included for the presentation to result in conversion?

3. Which gospel presentations presented do you think would work best in your community? Why?

Discussion Question

1. Summarize Keller's three-stage gospel presentation. Discuss what theological ideas each stage emphasizes and how. What are the reasons why this is a good gospel presentation?

Quiz

1. Which of the following does NOT exist in the Bible's various gospel presentations?

   a) The person and work of Jesus
   b) The blessings of the gospel
   c) The correct response to the gospel
   d) A systematic apologetic

2. Which of the following is NOT one of Blocher's main metaphors for "sin"?

   a) Transgression
   b) Falling short

    c) Impurity

    d) Iniquity

3. Which is NOT one of the theological components of sin?

    a) Internal

    b) Vertical

    c) Unilateral

    d) Horizontal

4. Which of the following is a component of God's judgment?

    a) Privation of good

    b) Internal

    c) Transgression

    d) The correct response to the gospel

5. Which of the following is one of the three biblical concepts of sin?

    a) Privation of good

    b) Defilement

    c) Vertical

    d) Transgression

6. Which of the following is NOT one of the three gospel presentations described?

    a) Two Ways to Live

    b) Life as a Wager

    c) Four Spiritual Laws

    d) The Bridge to Life

7. The chief gospel metaphor(s) used by Two Ways to Live is which of the following?

    a) God is King

    b) God is Lover

    c) The judgment for sin is separation from God

    d) The judgment for sin is punishment from God

    e) A & D

    f) All of the above

8. Which of the following is a weakness of Four Spiritual Laws?

   a) There is no joy in the Christian life — only submission
   b) It offers a platonized or spiritualized view of the material world
   c) It has little to say about the material world and what we do once we are saved
   d) The category of salvation-history is not so prominent

9. Which of the following is a strength of Bridge to Life?

   a) God is Creator
   b) Judgment is separation from God
   c) God is warm, personal, loving, and relational
   d) Judgment is a privation of good
   e) A & B
   f) A & C
   g) All of the above

10. Which theological idea is NOT discussed in Keller's gospel presentation?

   a) Incarnation
   b) Atonement
   c) Ascension
   d) Restoration

ANSWER KEY

1. D, 2. C, 3. C, 4. A, 5. B, 6. B, 7. E, 8. D, 9. E 10. C

CHAPTER 4

Evangelism to Postmoderns

You Should Know

- Epistemology: "How do we know something?"

- Don Carson's essential features of Modernity: knowledge begins with "I"; foundationalism; methods of knowing must be unbiased and objective; certainty of knowledge is possible; naturalism (matter is all that exists); truth is universal

- Postmodernity's refutations of modernity's epistemological features: subjectivity of the individual; coherentism instead of foundationalism; methods of knowing are biased and subjective; certainty of knowledge is impossible; naturalism is challenged; no universal truth

- Postmodernism's evangelism-assisting developments: tolerance is the highest moral good; all religions are valid and essentially the same; there are no absolutes; proof or evidence is unconvincing; there are diverse ways of knowing; open to the different perspectives of other cultures; ethics have become a barrier to belief in the gospel

- The assumption in modernity was that what is true, good, and beautiful is universal. The assumption in postmodernity is that what is true, good, and beautiful is determined by its context.

- Although we can't have absolute knowledge of the truth (only God can have this), we can know the truth nonetheless through our multiple perspectives.

- Authenticity: this is a postmodern buzzword; means one is living coherently with one's beliefs; holding true to oneself

- The major categories of knowledge in the Bible: providence, salvation-history, and wisdom

- Proposed postmodern pedagogical sequence: praxis, belief, truth

Reflection Questions

1. Explain how a pyramid structure of knowledge works. How do you see this in how your church presents the gospel message?

2. How do you engage in evangelism in a postmodern world? What do you need to know to evaluate how to best share the gospel in this context?

3. Do you agree that wisdom can be an entry point into the gospel? Why or why not? How might wisdom be applied successfully to a gospel presentation?

Discussion Question

1. Summarize the age of postmodernity. Describe how postmodernity interacts with Carson's epistemological features of modernity.

Quiz

1. (T/F) Epistemology refers to the "how" of knowing — i.e., "how do we know something?"

2. (T/F) René Descartes marked the shift from the medieval age to pre-modernity.

3. (T/F) Descartes's famous axiom is "I doubt, therefore I am."

4. Which of the following refers to everything one believes and how these beliefs relate with each other?

    a) Empiricism
    b) Rationalism

    c) Coherentism

    d) Foundationalism

5. (T/F) According to Carson, postmodernity is a reaction against the epistemological assumptions of modernity.

6. (T/F) In postmodernism, truth is objective and external to the person.

7. The buzzword for postmodernists is "_____."

    a) Subjectivity

    b) Universality

    c) Objectivity

    d) Authenticity

8. Which of the following is NOT one of the Bible's major categories of knowledge?

    a) Providence

    b) Salvation-history

    c) Revelation

    d) Wisdom

9. Which pedagogical sequence would be better suited for postmoderns?

    a) Truth > belief > praxis

    b) Praxis > belief > truth

    c) Belief > praxis > truth

    d) Praxis > truth > belief

10. (T/F) With postmodern listeners, preachers need to spend more time on application than on exposition.

ANSWER KEY

1. T, 2. F, 3. F, 4. D, 5. T, 6. F, 7. D, 8. C, 9. B, 10. T

CHAPTER 5

Contextualization for Evangelism

You Should Know

- Syncretism: a merger of one's own culture with the gospel

- Examples of idiomatic language: "Take a seat."; "I want to ride shotgun!"; "What's up?"; and "Go for your life!"

- When we over-adapt to a culture, we tend towards syncretism. When we under-adapt to a culture, we tend towards legalism.

- James Sire's key questions for discovering a culture's worldview: "Who am I?"; "Where am I?"; "What's wrong?"; and "What is the solution?"

- Simon Smart's six themes for discovering a culture's worldview: reality, human nature, death, knowing, values, purpose

- Keller's three parts to discovering a culture's storyline: the way things should be; something that stops this from happening; something that achieves the mission

- Steps in the task of contextualization: interpreting the gospel; communicating the gospel; applying the gospel

- The aim of contextualization is to have a dialogue between the cultures of the three major players in evangelism: our own culture, the culture of the Bible, and the culture of the hearer.

Reflection Questions

1. Summarize how the audience being enculturated affects how the gospel message is received. Share using examples, if possible.

2. Summarize how you can interpret a culture through its themes. What are some themes evident in your culture, and how might these impact a gospel presentation?

3. Summarize the threefold task of contextualization in your own words.

Discussion Question

1. Outline the various methods discussed for interpreting a culture (cultural hermeneutics).

Quiz

1. A merger of one's own culture with the gospel is called _____.
   a) Sacerdotalism
   b) Synergy
   c) Asyndotalism
   d) Syncretism

2. (T/F) Many Christians impose their culture, along with the gospel, as if it is normative and universal.

3. (T/F) The gospel is acultural.

4. (T/F) The gospel will be applied equally in each culture.

5. (T/F) There are forms of gospel presentation that hover above culture.

6. We tend towards legalism when we _____ to a culture.
   a) Over-adapt
   b) Over-empathize
   c) Under-adapt
   d) Under-empathize

7. Which of the following is NOT one of James Sire's worldview-discovering questions?
   a) "Who am I?"
   b) "What is the solution?"

c) "What's wrong?"

d) "Who did it?"

8. Which of the following is NOT one of Simon Smart's worldview themes?

a) Reality

b) Life

c) Knowing

d) Values

9. Which of the following is NOT one of Keller's cultural storylines?

a) The way things used to be

b) Something that stops this from happening

c) The way things should be

d) Something that achieves the mission

10. The aim of contextualization is to have a _____ between the cultures of the three major players in evangelism.

a) Synchronic understanding

b) Diachronic understanding

c) Excursus

d) Dialogue

ANSWER KEY

1. D, 2. T, 3. F, 4. F, 5. F, 6. C, 7. D, 8. B, 9. A, 10. D

CHAPTER 6

Gospel-Cultural Hermeneutics

You Should Know

- Cultural texts: culturally produced works that communicate meaning and call for interpretation

- Gospel-cultural hermeneutics: interpreting a cultural text through the lenses of the gospel

- The steps in entering a culture's storyline: Read the "text" on its own terms and describe it; understand it; empathize with it.

- The W Spectrum: Workers show how Christ *triumphs over* their culture; workers show how Christ *replaces* their culture; workers show how Christ *transforms* people in their culture; workers show how Christ *completes* their culture.

- Examples of W1 of the W Spectrum: oppose the culture's storyline; "your culture's storyline is wrong"; Christ triumphs over your culture's storyline; transgression or rebellion

- Examples of W4 of the W Spectrum: invite people to follow Jesus within their culture's storyline; "your culture's storyline is heading in the right direction"; Christ fulfills your culture's storyline; falling short

- To be kept in mind when practicing gospel-cultural hermeneutics: Demonstrate understanding and empathy for the cultural storyline; use language, idioms, and metaphors from that culture; identify the universal, existential cry for love and belonging; show Jesus as the true fulfillment of the cultural storyline without forcing it.

- The more we universalize our message, the less it will be contextualized.

Reflection Questions

1. What does it mean to understand a cultural text in terms of using it as evangelism? Explain how the tool of gospel-cultural hermeneutics works to contextualize the gospel to an audience's culture.

2. Explain how Paul fulfilled the storyline of his culture in Acts 17:16–34. What might this process look like in your own community and culture?

3. What are some strengths to universalizing the gospel message? What are some weaknesses?

Discussion Question

1. Describe each of the four steps in the W Spectrum. Explain how to apply the W Spectrum in your own context.

Quiz

1. (T/F) Gospel-cultural hermeneutics involves interpreting a cultural text through the lenses of the gospel.

2. Cultures produce works of meaning — "_____" — that both communicate meaning and call for interpretation.

   a) Cultural texts
   b) Transcultural texts
   c) Acultural texts
   d) Cultural storylines

3. Which of the following is NOT one of the steps in entering a culture's storyline?

   a) Speak the gospel
   b) Empathize with it

    c) Understand it

    d) Read the "text" on its own terms and describe it

4. A step for understanding is concerned with finding the God-given
_____ within a culture's storyline.

    a) Cultural text

    b) Existential cry

    c) Chief motif

    d) Metaphor

5. Which step correlates to challenging a culture's storyline?

    a) Speak the gospel

    b) Understand it

    c) Deconstruct it

    d) How does the Gospel answer this existential cry and storyline

6. (T/F) The Mason Jar is dissonant because it can't deliver what it promises.

7. (T/F) Speaking the gospel is a step in entering a culture's storyline.

8. Which W model correlates with showing how Christ replaces their culture?

    a) W1

    b) W2

    c) W3

    d) W4

9. (T/F) The W3 model emphasizes how Christ transforms people in their culture.

10. (T/F) The more we universalize our message, the more it will be contextualized.

ANSWER KEY

1. T, 2. A, 3. A, 4. B, 5. C, 6. F, 7. F, 8. B, 9. T, 10. F

CHAPTER 7

Storytelling the Gospel

You Should Know

- Abstract learning: learning which begins with theoretical concepts which are then applied

- Concrete-relational learning: learning which begins with stories of how things work, and from that a theory is abstracted.

- Abstract learners tend to be literate learners, while concrete-relational learners tend to be oral learners.

- Stories ask the listener to suspend disbelief appropriate to the genre of storytelling.

- SAM: simple; accurate; memorable

- Questions for generating discussion: What impressed you about the story itself? What questions do you want answered from the story? What does the story teach us about people? What does the story teach us about Jesus (or God)? What is God teaching you from this story?

- Steps for using storytelling to tell the gospel: Choose a story from the Bible; read the passage carefully several times; re-tell the passage in your own words; practice re-telling the story to another person.

- Guidelines for generating discussion in formal situations: Tell audience this is an exercise in post-literate learning; ask what impressed them about the story; have them discuss it in pairs; have them share their answers with the whole group.

Reflection Questions

1. What are the two different types of learning? How does the Bible use both styles of learning? Give some examples of each one and why they work for that particular style of learning.

2. In your experience, do people prefer a dialogue or a monologue for learning? Why? How might you adapt your evangelism techniques to reflect the audience preference?

3. What are some strengths and weaknesses of the storytelling method?

Discussion Question

1. Summarize the author's preferred method for using storytelling to communicate the gospel. What is the acronym used for remembering his storytelling guidelines, and what does it stand for?

Quiz

1. (T/F) People who prefer abstract learning begin with stories of how things work, and from that they abstract a theory.

2. Abstract learners are _____ learners.
   a) Literate
   b) Oral
   c) Concrete-relational
   d) Explanatory

3. Concrete-relational learners are _____ learners.
   a) Literate
   b) Oral
   c) Concrete-relational
   d) Explanatory

4. (T/F) When learning to re-tell a story from the Bible in your own words, it's unnecessary to memorize the story word-for-word.

5. Which of the following is NOT one of the guidelines for re-telling a biblical story?

   a) Simple
   b) Accurate
   c) Manageable
   d) Memorable

6. Which is the acronym for learning how to tell a story from the Bible?

   a) MAS
   b) MSA
   c) AMS
   d) SAM

7. Which of the following is NOT one of the questions for generating group discussion?

   a) What impressed you about the story itself?
   b) What do you think the story was about?
   c) What does the story teach us about people?
   d) What is God teaching you from this story?

8. (T/F) According to the author, people prefer a monologue over a dialogue.

9. (T/F) Based on experience, the storytelling model works best if you have at least one-third Christians in the group.

10. (T/F) Storytelling has the added benefit of explaining complex theological concepts without complicated language.

ANSWER KEY

1. F, 2. A, 3. B, 4. T, 5. C, 6. D, 7. B, 8. F, 9. F, 10. T

CHAPTER 8

How to Give Evangelistic Topical Talks

You Should Know

- Dialogical or abductive approach: an approach to the Bible that acknowledges our presuppositions from the start

- The expository versus topical preaching debate is actually a question of pedagogy rather than theological orthodoxy.

- Steps for preparing a topical evangelistic talk: Move from the topic to a big idea; outline a bird's-eye view of the talk; explore the logical sequence of ideas in the body of the talk; flesh out the body of the talk.

- Sequence for generating a "big idea": topic, issue, argument (for a specific point)

- We know we have a good point if it answers the question raised by the issue, has an obvious opposite point, and can be supported by appeals to evidence and stories.

- The body of the talk's logical sequences of ideas: resonance, dissonance (or deficiency), the gospel as the answer or fulfillment

- The five building blocks of communication: state the idea, illustrate it, explain it, give an example, give a payload or application

- Concrete methods: illustration, example, payload/application

Reflection Questions

1. What is the difference between a topical talk and an expository Bible talk? What are some strengths and weaknesses of each type of talk?

2. Explain the difference between resonance and dissonance or deficiency. What is the purpose of each of these steps? Will the talk work with only one of these steps? Why or why not?

3. Summarize how the five building blocks of communication can be used in the dissonance sequence of an evangelistic talk. What are some strengths of this approach? What are some weaknesses?

Discussion Question

1. Reference the author's example of a topical talk, and write your own topical talk, drawing on all that you've learned from this session.

Quiz

1. (T/F) One argument against topical Bible talks is that it lets the Bible set the agenda.

2. (T/F) Utilizing a dialogical or abductive approach to the Bible means that we start out acknowledging our presuppositions.

3. (T/F) The expository versus topical preaching debate is actually a question of semantics rather than theological orthodoxy.

4. (T/F) The Bible itself is one big expository talk.

5. Which of the following is not one of the steps for preparing a topical evangelistic talk?
   a) Move from the topic to a big idea
   b) Outline a bird's-eye view of the talk
   c) Let the Bible dictate the message of your talk
   d) Explore the logical sequence of ideas in the body of the talk

6. (T/F) The sequence for generating a "big idea" is issue → topic → argument.

7. Which the following is one of the logical sequences of ideas for the body of the talk?
   a) Resonance
   b) Empathy

c) Defense
d) Equilibrium

8. What is true about the statement: "Many Asians cannot swim"?

a) This is a propositional truth claim
b) This is an analogy
c) This is concrete
d) This gives you something to imagine

9. Which of the following is not one of the "five building blocks of communication"?

a) Illustrate it
b) Give an example
c) Defend it
d) Give a payload or application

10. Which of the following is not one of the concrete or abstract methods that the author prefers to use?

a) State
b) Explain
c) Illustrate
d) Resonate

CHAPTER 9

How to Give Evangelistic Expository Talks

You Should Know

- In every "Bible talk" there is a dialectic between the two conceptual realms of the world of the text and the world of the hearer.

- Categories of "big ideas": exegetical, theological, homiletical, bumper sticker

- Big idea — *what?* Question — *why?* Existential question — *want?* Sinful problem — *need?* Gospel solution — *must?*

- Five things we do in an introduction to a talk or sermon: image, subject, need, pretext, preview

- The three-point options for a talk: unpack the big idea point by point; problem, solution, application; resonance, dissonance, gospel fulfillment

- The options for a three-point structure approach to narratival preaching: Retell the story, point by point; explain the story by unpacking the big idea, point by point; apply the story, point by point; the points are resonance, dissonance, gospel fulfillment.

- Elements of the body in the story-telling approach to narrative preaching: story-telling the story; asking three questions from the story; answering these three questions

- Formula for the Sinner's Prayer: Confess to the metaphor for sin in the talk; ask for the metaphor of salvation in the talk; thank God for the metaphor of Christ and his work in the talk.

Reflection Questions

1. Explain the three basic elements present in both topical and expository talks. What is each element's main purpose? (p. 187)

2. Summarize the five things we need to do in an introduction to a talk or sermon. How does each thing relate to the others?

3. What is the key for storytelling the narrative? What are some strengths of this approach? What are some weaknesses?

Discussion Question

1. Choose one passage from the lists in this section. Piece together the big idea (*what?*), question (*why?*), existential question (*want?*), sinful problem (*need?*), and gospel solution (*must?*).

Quiz

1. (T/F) In every "Bible talk" there is a dialectic between two conceptual realms: The world of the speaker and world of the hearer.

2. (T/F) The main difference between so-called "topical" and "expository" preaching is the proportion and sequencing of the elements.

3. Which of the following is not one of the basic elements present in all talks — "topical" and "expository"?

    a) Introduction
    b) Speaker's message
    c) Bible's message
    d) Application

4. Which of the following is one of the categories of big ideas?

    a) Topical
    b) Propositional
    c) Concrete
    d) Bumper sticker

5. The _____ big idea is the *what?* of the talk.

   a) Exegetical
   b) Theological
   c) Homiletical
   d) Bumper sticker

6. (T/F) The existential question is what gets us entry into the talk.

7. Which is NOT one of the things we do in an introduction?

   a) Image
   b) Subject
   c) Need
   d) Object

8. Which is NOT one of the options for the talk's three points?

   a) Unpack the big idea point-by-point
   b) Problem, solution, application
   c) Resonance, dissonance, gospel fulfillment
   d) Introduction, body, application

9. Which is NOT one of the options for a three-point structure approach to narratival preaching?

   a) Retell the story, point-by-point
   b) Explain the story by unpacking the big idea, point-by-point
   c) The points are resonance, dissonance, gospel fulfillment
   d) Problem, solution, application

10. (T/F) The conclusion usually has a bumper sticker idea for the audience.

ANSWER KEY

1. F, 2. T, 3. B, 4. D, 5. C, 6. T, 7. D, 8. D, 9. D, 10. T

CHAPTER 10

Religious Epistemology, Apologetics, and Defeater Beliefs

You Should Know

- Religious epistemology: "Why do some people believe in the existence of God, but others don't?"

- *Logos* — what I say; *pathos* — the way I make you feel; *ethos* — the way I live

- People tend to believe what trusted people (doctors, spouses, parents, scientists, etc.) tell them.

- *Pathos* and *ethos* are chronologically prior to *logos*.

- Cumulative case method: jettisoning our worldview for another worldview that better accommodates the new evidence based on continual analysis and consistent results

- Evidentialism: the apologetic approach that believes that if we give people evidence for what we believe then this evidence will compel them to belief

- Presuppositionalism: the apologetic approach that presumes the Christian presuppositions and starts from there

- Three-point process for addressing defeater beliefs: resonate, dismantle, gospel

- A hard theodicy will try to specify the reasons God has for allowing suffering. A soft theodicy will say that God has reasons for allowing suffering, but we don't know what they are.

Reflection Questions

1. How might understanding a culture's "defeater beliefs" make evangelism more effective in today's culture? Compare the early church with today's church with this process.

2. In your opinion, does the church today do a good job of addressing the defeater belief of "What about other religions?" Why or why not?

3. Which type of apologetics appeals most to you and your community's culture? How could you adapt this chosen approach into your evangelism efforts?

Discussion Question

1. Summarize how to address the defeater belief in each of the examples using the three-part format (resonate, dismantle, gospel).

Quiz

1. Which ancient Greek component relates to what I say?

   a) *Logos*
   b) *Pathos*
   c) *Ethos*
   d) *Philos*

2. The _____ method involves jettisoning our worldview for another worldview that better accommodates the new evidence based on continual analysis and consistent results.

   a) Commutative
   b) Case-by-case
   c) Cumulative case
   d) Distributive

3. Which of the following is NOT part of modified presuppositional apologetic?

   a) Gospel
   b) Defend

c) Dismantle

d) Resonate

4. Another way to share the gospel is to show where the _____ is in the storyline and how the gospel resolves it.

   a) Deficiency

   b) Dissonance

   c) Resonance

   d) Difference

5. The three-point process we're using to answer today's defeater beliefs is:

   a) Introduction, body, application

   b) *Logos, pathos, ethos*

   c) Retell, explain, apply

   d) Resonate, dismantle, gospel

6. Which of the following is a presupposition of the belief that all religions are the same?

   a) God might be ephemeral and unknowable

   b) Hell is the opposite of tolerance and love

   c) We can only rationally believe what science can prove

   d) Everything we believe comes from science

7. Which of the following is NOT a presupposition of the belief that science disproves Christianity?

   a) Propositional truth claims are insufficient

   b) We can only rationally believe what science can prove

   c) Everything we believe comes from science

   d) Faith is anti-science

8. Which is a presupposition of the belief that Christians are judgmental hypocrites?

   a) Belief in objective truth is what brings out the worst in people

   b) The Bible says things that we would no longer hold to be true

   c) What the Bible says is objectionable

   d) The existence of evil disproves the existence of God

9. The problem of suffering only exists if we hold all of these truths to be true at the same time: (1) suffering is real, (2) suffering is unfair, (3) God is loving, and (4) _____.

    a) Jesus is God

    b) God is powerful

    c) Love means tolerating others

    d) God is supposed to make us happy

10. Which is one objection to the hard theodicy approach?

    a) It's hard to defend theologically

    b) It's hard to defend homiletically

    c) It's pastorally ignorant

    d) It's too hard to understand

ANSWER KEY

1. A, 2. C, 3. B, 4. B, 5. D, 6. A, 7. A, 8. A, 9. B, 10. A

Notes

www.ingramcontent.com/pod-product-compliance
Lightning Source LLC
Chambersburg PA
CBHW011746020426
42331CB00014B/3299